KAMLOOPS SECONDARY
SCHOOL LIBRARY

TWENTIETH-CENTURY DEVELOPMENTS IN FASHION AND COSTUME

FESTIVALS

Other books in this series include:

Military Uniforms
Carol Harris and Mike Brown

Accessories
Carol Harris and Mike Brown

Children's Costumes
Carol Harris and Mike Brown

Women's Costumes
Carol Harris and Mike Brown

Men's Costumes
Carol Harris and Mike Brown

North American Dress
Dr. Louise Aikman

Ceremonial Costumes
Lewis Lyons

The Performing Arts
Alycen Mitchell

Everyday Dress
Chris McNab

Rescue Services
Carol Harris and Mike Brown

Religious Costumes
Ellen Galford

TWENTIETH-CENTURY DEVELOPMENTS IN FASHION AND COSTUME

FESTIVALS

ELLEN GALFORD

MASON CREST PUBLISHERS
www.masoncrest.com

Mason Crest Publishers Inc.
370 Reed Road
Broomall, PA 19008
(866) MCP-BOOK (toll free)
www.masoncrest.com

Copyright © 2003 Amber Books Ltd.

All rights reserved. No part of this publication may be reproduced or transmitted in any form or by any means, electronic or mechanical, including photocopying, recording, taping, or any information storage and retrieval system, without permission in writing from the publisher.

First printing 2002

1 2 3 4 5 6 7 8 9 10

Library of Congress Cataloging-in-Publication Data available

ISBN 1-59084-423-8

Printed and bound in Malaysia

Editorial and design by
Amber Books Ltd.
Bradley's Close
74–77 White Lion Street
London N1 9PF

Project Editor: Marie-Claire Muir
Designer: Zoe Mellors
Picture Research: Lisa Wren

Picture Credits:
Corbis: 17. **The Culture Archive:** 22, 43, 45, 51. **Mary Evans Picture Library:** 12, 23, 27, 28, 37, 39. **Popperfoto:** 5 (all), 8, 11, 15, 18, 21, 30, 36, 50, 52–53, 55, 59. **Topham:** 6, 9, 33, 35, 40, 46, 44, 57.

Cover images: The Culture Archive: top right and bottom right. **Popperfoto:** background and main.

Acknowledgment:
For authenticating this book, the Publishers would like to thank
JONES NEW YORK.

Contents

Introduction   7

Chapter 1   9
Mardi Gras and Carnival

Chapter 2   23
Santa Claus

Chapter 3   37
Halloween

Chapter 4   51
Festivals Around the World

Glossary   60

Timeline   61

Further Information   62

Index   64

Introduction

Every day we go to our closets with the same question in mind: what shall I wear today? Clothing can convey status, wealth, occupation, religion, sexual orientation, and social, political, and moral values. The clothes we wear affect how we are perceived and also reflect what image we want to project.

Fashion has always been influenced by the events, people, and places that shape society. The 20th century was a period of radical change, encompassing two world wars, suffrage, a worldwide Depression, the invention of "talkies" and the rise of Hollywood, the birth of the teenager, the global spread of television, and, later, the World Wide Web, to name just a few important developments. Politically, economically, technologically, and socially, the world was changing at a fast and furious pace. Fashion, directly influenced by all these factors, changed with them, leaving each period with its fashion icon.

The 1920s saw the flapper reign supreme, with her short dress and cropped, boyish hair. The '30s and '40s brought a wartime mindset: women entered the workforce en masse and traded their silk stockings for nylon. During the conservative 1950s—typified by twin sets and capri pants—a young Elvis Presley took the world by storm. The '60s gave us PVC, miniskirts, and mods, and in 1967, the Summer of Love spawned a new language of fashion in which bell-bottoms and tie-dyed shirts became political expressions of peace and love. In the 1980s, power and affluence became the hallmarks of a new social group, the yuppies. Designer branding led the way, and the slogan "Nothing comes between me and my Calvins" started an era of status dressing. The 1990s will be best remembered for a new fashion word introduced by the underground street and music movement of Seattle, grunge.

Twentieth-Century Developments in Fashion and Culture is a 12-volume, illustrated series that looks at changing fashions throughout this eventful century, and encourages readers to question what the clothes they wear reveal about themselves and the world they live in.

Special introduction and consultation:
JONES NEW YORK

CHAPTER 1

Mardi Gras and Carnival

The Queen of England—complete with tiara, royal regalia, and a pair of high heels—sashays down Canal Street in New Orleans, moving to the beat of a marching band while shouts of "Long live the Queen!" rise from the crowded sidewalks.

The Queen gives a regal wave to the crowds lining the streets. They know she is actually a 6-foot- (183-cm-) tall man wearing a larger-than-life rubber mask, but they wave back anyway. Just behind Her Majesty come three former U.S. presidents,

Festooned with the strings of beads that Mardi Gras paraders throw to spectators, a New Orleans father and his sons hail the marchers and beg for more to add to their collection.

FESTIVALS

two Elvis Presleys, a gorilla wearing **crinolines** and a rhinestone tiara, a troop of aliens from an unknown galaxy, and Harry Potter. Some parade on their own, others in little groups of friends in carefully matched disguises. Still others, belonging to the carnival societies known as **krewes**, travel the route in formal processions, escorting floats swathed in green, gold, and purple bunting. Swaying under the weight of ornate headdresses and flashing millions of multicolored sequins, the krewes throw handfuls of trinkets to the crowd. Absolutely everyone is festooned with rope upon rope of glittery beads.

On this late-winter morning, visitors have flooded in from all over the world to celebrate alongside the citizens of Louisiana's largest and most colorful city. Some, armed with cameras, come only to watch and admire. But for those who join the masquerade, no costume idea is too outrageous. Some will have spent all year creating the most spectacular disguises that their imaginations can invent or money can buy—because this is the celebration when the good times roll and almost anything goes. This is Mardi Gras!

Mardi Gras in French means "Fat Tuesday." The name marks that day in the religious calendar when, traditionally, **pious** Christians enjoy their last taste of meat and other rich foods before the six-week period of **abstinence** known as Lent. But the people of New Orleans are not the only ones who use the eve of this solemn fast as the perfect excuse for an end-of-winter festival. In Europe, Latin America, and the Caribbean, the same festival goes under the name of Carnival, from the Latin words *carne vale*—literally, "farewell to meat."

ANCIENT ORIGINS

Some historians believe that the roots of Carnival go further back than the beginnings of the Christian faith. The inhabitants of ancient Rome also took the opportunity to light up the darkest season of the year with a raucous holiday. On the feast of **Saturnalia**, the usual rules of society were suspended. Fun, feasting, and mischief became the order of the day. Even slaves, for a few

MARDI GRAS AND CARNIVAL

These gilded masks and luxurious costumes worn at the Carnival in Venice pay tribute to stock characters from the Italian Renaissance theatrical tradition known as the *Commedia dell' Arte*.

short, intoxicating hours, might find themselves trading places with their masters, free to play tricks that would get them into serious trouble any other time of the year.

MEDIEVAL EUROPE

Other scholars doubt that there is a connection—beyond the need to let off steam and find some excuse for celebration in such dark days—between these pagan revels and the Carnivals that have taken place in many parts of Christian Europe since the Middle Ages. These festivals first appeared in the record books

The ladies at this 19th-century Carnival ball dress in fashionable but conventional finery, while their male companions caper in outlandish masks and bizarre disguises.

> **CARNIVAL DIGNITARIES**
>
> Typically, every Carnival also had its kings, queens, and courtiers. In some localities, the individuals who temporarily wielded the scepters and wore the gilded crowns were local dignitaries or wealthy merchants, who had paid high sums for the right to take these roles. Sometimes, the rulers of Carnival were those folk who spent the rest of the year mending shoes or cleaning out **latrines**. Whatever their social status, the lucky candidates did their best to look the part. This was the one day in the year when the world was turned upside down. Over the centuries, it became the custom to use Carnival as an ideal opportunity to make fun of those local townspeople who held positions of power. In the Carnival held in 1795 in the town of Montmorillon, for instance, the general public disguised themselves as sheep, while the tax collectors dressed as wolves.

in the 14th century. In medieval France, Switzerland, Italy, and Germany, masks and costumes played an important part in the event. Sometimes, the disguises consisted of nothing more than a few rags and a mixture of mud, flour, and ashes that peasants and poor townspeople daubed on their faces to give themselves the terrifying appearance of ghosts and demons.

Others indulged in more elaborate masquerades. During the Carnivals held in the French town of Romans in the 1580s, members of the upper classes marched in processions wearing the vividly colored and patterned uniform of the Swiss Guards—the same **venerable** military unit that today patrols Vatican City in Rome protecting the Pope. Men dressed as bears and wolves capered through the streets. Some of those inside these hairy suits did their best to imitate those creatures' wild behavior by frightening children or pursuing any young maidens who came within range.

FESTIVALS

FROM PARIS TO NEW ORLEANS

The traditional ways in which 18th-century Parisians bade their annual "farewell" to meat and other things became a source of inspiration to their like-minded cousins and one-time colonists across the Atlantic Ocean. New Orleans, as part of a vast tract of North American territory known as the Louisiana Purchase, eventually passed from French hands into the ownership of the United States in 1803. However, this change in nationality did not lead automatically to a change in culture. The people of New Orleans saw no reason to abandon the Old World tradition of dressing up at Carnival time. The upper classes marked the festival with private masquerade parties and balls, while the rest of the population took to the streets. In 1835, for example, a visitor named John Creecy reported masqueraders rampaging through the town in bizarre disguises: "Human bodies are seen with heads of beasts and birds! Snakes' heads and bodies with arms of apes; man-bats from the moon; mermaids, **satyrs**, beggars, monks, and robbers."

If the costumes were alarming, the revelers' rowdy behavior was even more so. By the 1850s, there was talk of banning Mardi Gras. However, a group of pleasure-loving and public-spirited citizens came up with an alternative. They proposed a well-organized and carefully controlled celebration featuring a formal torchlight procession. The first of these parades began in 1857, and after 1872, each festival had its presiding King, a leading citizen crowned and robed in the style of a medieval monarch.

Since then, the event has evolved in ways that reflect the rich ethnic and racial composition of a place that is often described as the least American of all American cities. Nevertheless, as in so many urban centers, the white and black populations of New Orleans have traditionally inhabited different neighborhoods and lived more or less separate lives. Although the civil-rights reforms of the 1960s brought an end to legally imposed **segregation**, the two communities have chosen to develop separate Mardi Gras organizations. Their parades, which take place in different parts of the city center, display their own distinctive styles of music and costume.

KREWES

Traditionally, the festivities within the white community are dominated by the official Mardi Gras societies, known as krewes. The oldest of these groups draws its members from the city's wealthiest and most prominent male inhabitants, many of whom trace their ancestry back to the old French colonial elite. Each krewe, ruled by a King, conducts its own formal procession through the streets, escorting lavishly decorated floats. They march in formation behind their captain, a mysterious figure who rides a tall horse and conceals his face behind a jewel-studded piece of cloth. Although certain krewes still cling to their customary exclusivity, newer carnival societies, welcoming a more diverse range of members, have added to the mix. Some even look outside New Orleans for their Kings, choosing national celebrities or high-profile politicians to head the parade.

Ermine cuffs and a gold, gem-encrusted crown and tunic give Rex, official King of Mardi Gras, a regal appearance. Enthroned upon a float and escorted by his krewe, he parades along Canal Street in New Orleans.

FESTIVALS

THE FIRST FEMALE KREWE
The appearance of the first female krewe in 1922 came at a time when women throughout the Western world were fighting for their civil rights. In that year, a group of upper-class New Orleans ladies formed the Iris Krewe, naming their society after the ancient Greek goddess of the rainbow. On their first outing, the members dressed in modest, richly colored gowns that reflected all the colors of their patron deity. As time and attitudes moved on, this particular krewe's costumes have stayed just as bright, but have become considerably less demure. In 1987, for example, the followers of Iris sported thigh-skimming fringed microskirts and figure-hugging tunics ablaze with sequins and spangles.

SATIRE AND SOCIAL CHANGE
Following an old Mardi Gras tradition, many krewes choose an annual theme and design their costumes, masks, and floats around it. Sometimes, the topic is **satirical**. One early example occurred in 1877. At the time, the disgruntled citizens expressed their disapproval for President Ulysses S. Grant by choosing the theme of Hades, the ancient Greek version of hell. A little over a century later, when the Americans were involved in the Gulf War, the carnival krewes went into a patriotic mode when they directed their satire against the Iraqi leader Saddam Hussein.

Satire also inspired the black community's Mardi Gras societies. In 1909, an African American named William Storey decided to mock the white aristocrats who vied with each other to reign as King over the official celebrations. He appointed courtiers and led his own march through the black neighborhoods, wearing a battered tin can on his head in a teasing imitation of the white King's elaborate crown.

MARDI GRAS AND CARNIVAL

MARDI GRAS "INDIANS"

Today, the black societies, known as the "Mardi Gras Indian tribes," have become world-famous for their dramatic and richly inventive costumes, and their parades provide a visually stunning climax to the city's celebrations. While the traditional costumes of the white krewes are based on romantic notions about medieval court fashions, those of the "Indians" spring from an idealized version of Native American dress, embellished and transformed into unique works of art.

The essential elements of the "Indian" costume include a massive feathered headdress and suit consisting of leggings and a huge apron-like garment covered with lavishly decorated, hand-embroidered panels called plaques. The images on these panels range from realistic pictures of horses, birds, rattlesnakes, and Indian

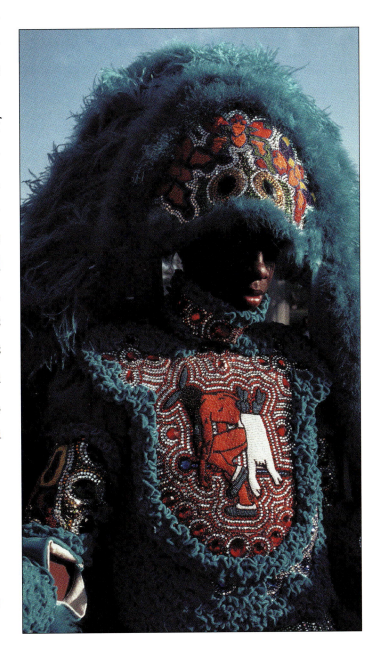

This Carnival reveler wears an elaborate, feathered headdress that is typical of the "Indian" costume. The plaque on his chest has been exquisitely decorated.

FESTIVALS

heroes to floral patterns and complicated abstract designs. Present-day plaques are made of such materials as velvet, lace, ribbons, rhinestones, sequins, and beads. In earlier times, the "Indians," having no money for such frivolous objects, used their creativity instead. To create color and sparkle, they pieced together old bottle caps, pieces of broken glass, even fragments of eggshells.

The full **regalia** can weigh as much as 150 pounds (68 kg). Measured from the top of his furred and feathered headdress, the tribal leader may rise to a height of 8 feet (244 cm) or more, towering over the crowd. Year after year, the costumes become more fantastic as each Chief strives to outdo and amaze his rivals from the city's other tribes. Some veteran Chiefs, however, worry about the future. The cost of creating a Mardi Gras Indian costume can run into thousands of dollars, and the time it takes to make one—especially for people on low pay with families to support—is an even scarcer resource.

To add to the dazzle of Sydney's (Australia) world-famous Gay and Lesbian Mardi Gras parade, a craftswoman labors to perfect a female figure sculpted from styrofoam.

MARDI GRAS AND CARNIVAL

> **THE INDIAN CHIEF**
>
> It is a point of honor for the Chief of each tribe to design and construct his own costume, keeping the plans as secret as possible and allowing technical and financial help only from his closest relatives and most trusted friends. Unlike the King of the mainstream Mardi Gras, whose garments are the work of a team of professional costume designers and craftspeople, no self-respecting Chief would allow outsiders to intervene.
>
> "My costume," exclaims Larry Bannock, Chief of the Golden Star Hunters tribe, "is me! Making an Indian suit comes from your heart."

While "Indian" tribes and krewes dominate the formal parades, Mardi Gras in New Orleans would not be what it is today without another group of Carnival-goers—those individuals who invent their own weird and wonderful costumes. They take to the streets in between the scheduled processions, or strut on the sidewalks as the krewes and tribes go by: giant ballet-dancing frogs, **caricatures** of world leaders in outsized rubber masks, extraterrestrials, wizards, and Little Bo-Peep. They belong to no official society, but they represent a spirit of Carnival even older than the city's most venerable krewe.

MARDI GRAS AROUND THE WORLD

The New Orleans Mardi Gras is unforgettable, but it is certainly not unique. It is not even the only one of its kind in the United States. Other Louisiana towns have their own local celebrations. In Alabama, residents of the Gulf Coast seaport of Mobile have been marking the occasion just as long as their counterparts in New Orleans. In fact, there are those Alabamians who claim that the first New Orleans Mardi Gras krewe owed its existence to a group of young men from Mobile, who imported the idea from their old hometown.

FESTIVALS

DIRTY MAS

On the Caribbean island of Trinidad, the costumes are as diverse as the local population—a rich ethnic and religious mix, with roots in Africa, India, the Middle East, Great Britain, and Spain. The custom of "Mas," or masquerading, goes through two different phases, each with its own style of dressing up or down. The first of these, known as the "Dirty Mas," takes place in the early hours of Carnival Monday. Out of the darkness come eerie figures, in blue paint, sometimes half-naked, sporting devil's horns and tails and carrying pitchforks, or wearing other forms of grotesque disguise, with exaggerated physical features and **gargoyle** masks. The figures of the "Dirty Mas" disappear after sunrise, making way for the "Pretty Mas," when Carnival societies, or "Mas Bands," numbering 1,000 members or more, display their brilliantly colorful and ingenious costumes.

Each Mas Band dresses according to its chosen imagery for the year, with its King and Queen displaying the most extreme version of the idea, attended by **courtiers** in less-dramatic variations. The inspiration for these costumes comes from a variety of sources: folklore; flowers, birds, and insects; the realm of the dead (and the undead); satires on celebrities and politicians; history; mythology; and literature.

The most dramatic features of the Trinidadian Mas disguises are their size, scale, and technical complexity. They have moving parts, such as long, thrashing dragon tails, butterfly wings, flashing eyes, and fantastic limbs. The Trinidadian passion for costumes that are more like machines reached its peak in the 1960s and 1970s, when Carnival Kings were dragging around 200 pounds (91 km) of costume, and one Mas Band Queen reported that the weight of her **raiments** caused her to weep from the pain. By the 1980s, Trinidadian designers were using lighter synthetic materials.

MARDI GRAS AND CARNIVAL

The custom of parading through the streets in disguise can be seen the entire world over at Carnival time. But the costumes vary from country to country, and even from town to town. Differences in climate, culture, and history make their mark. Many of those dancing through the streets at Brazil's world-famous Carnival in Rio de Janeiro—where February temperatures can reach well above 80°F (27°C)—wear costumes constructed of lacy webs of beads, lacework, and feathery fringes.

But while sweating, suntanned Brazilians samba the sultry Carnival nights away, masqueraders in the German city of Munich find themselves caught in the icy grip of winter. Cloaks with fur collars, thick layers of face paint, and giant wigs that seem to have a life of their own, as well as huge hats made of plumage gathered from a variety of different birds, are essential for those who hope to enjoy the event without developing pneumonia.

These Brazilian revelers have a colorful fringe of feathers decorating their two-piece skirts.

21

CHAPTER 2

Santa Claus

It is a common misconception that the figure of Santa Claus familiar to people today is almost as old as Christmas itself. Instead, he is entirely an American invention, going back no more than a few generations, although his origins are ancient and international.

The bearded old man in the red suit carrying a sack of presents on his back is a familiar sight on every continent. His picture turns up everywhere. You can find him on a life-sized cardboard cutout in a London department store window, on a calendar stuck to the

The plump, leather-booted, red-suited Santa Claus (left) was devised by advertising artist Haddon Sundblom in 1931 for Coca-Cola. He is much more friendly than the austere St. Nicholas (right) represented in a Dutch illustration from the 1930s.

wall of a Himalayan mountain hut, and on several million greeting cards moving through post offices all across the United States at Christmas time at the end of every year.

SANTA'S FAMILY TREE

The modern-day Santa Claus is a recent addition to an ancient and diverse group of traditional gift-bringers. Some of these go back to pagan traditions older than Christianity. In Finnish Lapland, the embodiment of the midwinter festival was a supernatural horned goat called Joulupukki. The Norse peoples of Scandinavia believed that the bearded god-king, Odin, flew across the winter skies, his journey tracing an arc across the heavens. Instead of traveling in a sleigh drawn by airborne reindeer, Odin rode a dazzling white horse with eight legs. Just as children today leave out Christmas Eve snacks of milk or hot chocolate and cookies for Santa and his reindeer, Odin's worshippers provided a handful of sweet hay to feed their god's hungry horse. However, there was nothing cheerful about the bearded Norse god. Unlike the eagerly awaited Santa Claus, Odin inspired reverence, dread, and awe.

BEFANA

Generally, traditional Christmas-time gift-bearers are male, but in Italy, the traditional dispenser of holiday treats is female—a grey-haired, wrinkled old lady called La Befana. According to one version of her legend, La Befana gave shelter to the Three Kings during their journey, heard about the birth of Jesus, and set out alone to deliver her own much humbler presents to the miraculous baby. She never found her way to Bethlehem and has roamed the world ever since, filling good children's stockings with candy and bad children's stockings with coal.

Other less-terrifying northern European figures include Norway's red-capped gnome called Julenisse, and Russia's snowy-bearded, long-haired patriarch named Grandfather Frost. Father Christmas, who in parts of the English-speaking world is now identified as Santa Claus under another name, originally began life as someone completely different. He goes back at least as far as the 14th century, when he is mentioned in an early English play. The surviving text tells us nothing about his physical appearance, apart from the fact that he is an old man.

In parts of southern Europe, the holiday season is personified by characters associated with the New Testament nativity story. The Three Wise Men who have delivered toys to generations of Hispanic children are the same Three Kings who came from the East, following a mysterious star and bearing precious gifts for the infant Jesus. In Italy, the traditional dispenser of holiday treats is female—a grey-haired, wrinkled old lady called La Befana, who gave shelter to the Three Kings during their journey.

The Santa Claus we know today has some of the same traits as these other Christmas-time figures. For example, he rides through the sky like Odin, wears red headgear like Julenisse, has hair and beard as snowy as Grandfather Frost's, and, like Father Christmas, he is elderly and male. In the manner of La Befana, Santa Claus brings not only treats for the well-behaved, but also lumps of coal for those children who have misbehaved.

SAINT NICHOLAS

One of the most important names on the modern Santa's family tree is a Turkish saint named Nicholas, a bishop of the early Christian church. Nicholas is thought to have lived in the fourth century, but the only information about his life comes from a biography written 500 years later. It is impossible to know what facts its author, another saint named Methodius, had at his disposal, but he depicted Nicholas as a kindly miracle worker, a perfect candidate for the role of patron saint and protector of young children (he is also the patron saint for mariners and pawnbrokers).

In the Netherlands, Saint Nicholas has reigned for centuries as the central figure of the Christmas season. As Sinterklaas, he arrives, supposedly from Spain, in early December. He rides a white horse and is dressed in red robes and the regalia of a Catholic bishop. He wears a tall, pointed hat, called a miter, on his head and carries a crosier, a symbolic shepherd's crook expressing his role as guide and protector of his Christian flock.

SANTA IN THE NEW WORLD

In the 17th century, settlers from the Netherlands crossed the Atlantic Ocean. They established their colony of New Amsterdam on the site of present-day New York City. As immigrants do in any time or place, they brought their customs and traditions with them. So their beloved Sinterklaas came, too. But it would take almost 300 years before the ancient saint gave up his religious vestments and his horse, altered his face and figure, and entered the American imagination as Santa Claus. This was no overnight transformation. The change came gradually. And once it was complete, Santa owed his new identity as much to Chicago advertising agencies and New York department stores as to Old World legends of saints and pagan gods.

In 1809, long after English had replaced Dutch as the language spoken on the banks of the Hudson River in New York, the writer Washington Irving—famed creator of *Rip Van Winkle* and the terrifying headless horseman of *Sleepy Hollow*—looked back nostalgically to the now-distant days of New Amsterdam. He was inspired by the old colonial tales and traditions and painted his own portrait of Saint Nicholas. In his version, the saint flew over the rooftops in broad daylight, with presents crammed into the pockets of his old-fashioned **breeches**. He delivered these presents to each house by dropping them down the chimney onto the hearth.

A magazine from December 1930 depicts St. Nicholas in bishop's crown and robes, arriving by boat in the Netherlands. His traditional escort, Black Peter, wears a jacket and cap in the same red and white.

Fourteen years later, in 1823, the poet Clement Clark Moore made a few important adjustments to this image when he wrote *The Night Before Christmas*. First, he provided a new mode of transportation—the sleigh drawn by reindeer. But he also made Saint Nicholas' job much harder. Instead of dropping presents down the chimney, the great man now had to climb down it to deliver them by hand. Fortunately, the saint had not yet grown particularly fat. The poet described him as "little," although he did have a round face and

FESTIVALS

Thomas Nast, a famous American cartoonist of the late 19th century, illustrated Santa in a tight, wooly garment, resembling a set of long winter underwear. He also shows Santa using the latest piece of new technology—a telephone.

potbelly. The snowy beard had not reached its full growth, being no more than a scanty fringe of white chin-whiskers. He wore fur from head to toe, although the descent through various chimneys had smeared his clothing with ashes and soot. However, these stains did not spoil his good mood—his eyes sparkled and he showed dimples when he smiled.

It was in the 1860s when Santa Claus first acquired a face much like the one he wears today, courtesy of the newspaper cartoonist Thomas Nast. Famous for his savage caricatures of corrupt politicians, Nast first used the round, white-bearded countenance associated with today's Santa to depict Bacchus, the Greek god of wine and wild celebrations. In 1866, Nast recycled these same features to create a drawing of Santa Claus. He also decided to stick a pipe in Santa's mouth and place a jaunty, pointed cap on his head, as well as give him a one-piece suit in red fur.

GOOD FOR BUSINESS

By the closing years of the 19th century, Santa Claus was a familiar figure on city streets, asking for money on behalf of various good causes. Some New York charity collectors still dressed up as old Saint Nicholas, with his bishop's robes and miter; but others preferred the modern look of a scarlet-coated Santa carrying a sackful of toys.

This new-style Santa did not limit his fund-raising activities to the sick and the poor. He found a new role, putting his image to work on behalf of American businesses. And his image continued to evolve. In 1897, he advertised Pears soap wearing a broad belt and a cap. By 1902, advertisements for Waterman fountain pens showed him in a tailored suit of trousers and belted jacket with big, shiny leather boots and a generous head of hair. In the following year, the makers of Shredded Wheat took advantage of Santa's fame as a gift-giver, using him to tell the public that their cereal products were "The Greatest Food Gift to Man." The artwork depicted him as slimmer than the present-day Santa.

SANTA IN THE AMERICAN MEDIA

In 1912, Santa Claus made a significant leap from the advertising pages to the cover of one of America's most popular magazines. In that year, the Christmas edition of the *Saturday Evening Post* displayed a skinny street-corner charity collector wearing enormous Santa Claus robes. Painted by the illustrator J.C. Leyendecker, it launched a holiday tradition that would flourish for many decades.

FESTIVALS

Leyendecker's artwork for the 1918 Christmas issue reflected the preoccupations of the day. In solidarity with American soldiers fighting in World War I, that year's Santa wore a khaki uniform and an army helmet. By 1923, when peace and prosperity reigned once again, Leyendecker made Santa larger than life, dressing him in an opulent suit of velvet and fur, and putting a huge pair of laced leather boots on his oversized feet. The figure held a small child perched upon his knee and had a luminous circle—reminiscent of a halo—behind his head. Once he had created these images, Leyendecker used them elsewhere. His *Saturday Evening Post* Santa turned up as advertising artwork selling Kuppenheimer overcoats.

The Father Christmas figure depicted on this Victorian-era Christmas card sports a long, snow-white beard and has a sack full of toys. However, he wears a blue robe, not the red robe that is now traditionally associated with Santa Claus.

Within a few years, Leyendecker found himself competing for the *Saturday Evening Post* assignments with another illustrator, the artist Norman Rockwell. Rockwell had branched out to create Santa Claus with a different twist. Throughout the 1920s, he added a new dimension to Santa's identity. The face was entirely familiar—chubby-cheeked, white-bearded, and with a cherubic expression—but Rockwell showed him as a multidimensional, human character, resting at home after his Christmas toil or busy in the workshop preparing for the following year.

Santa's clothing in these pictures presented his ordinary, everyday side. Instead of his official fur-trimmed sleigh-riding suit, Santa relaxed in comfortable old clothes, looking like anybody's grandfather enjoying his cozy fireside. When Rockwell showed him supervising his pre-Christmas toy-making operations, he gave him the same businesslike green eyeshade worn throughout America by bookkeepers, newspaper editors, and other deskbound workers of the day.

SUNDBLOM'S SANTA

While Rockwell continued fleshing out Santa's personality, another illustrator completed the work of turning him into a national and global icon. Haddon Sundblom was a Chicago-based commercial artist who created advertising for such high-profile brands as Aunt Jemima pancake mix and Nabisco cereals. In 1931, the makers of Coca-Cola commissioned him to create a Santa Claus for their Christmas advertising campaign. The clients were so pleased with what he did that they continued to commission at least one new Santa advertisement annually for the next 33 years.

Sundblom's Santa Claus set the standard for all the images that followed. His most significant features were his enormous size, his large belly, his rosy cheeks, jovial expression, and the lush colors and luxuriant trimmings of his costume.

FESTIVALS

A SANTA IN EVERY STORE

While his painted image appeared in Coca-Cola's posters and advertisements, Santa Claus' costumed duplicates were busy in the flesh, drumming up trade in the nation's department stores. The father of all retail Santas was a New Englander named James Edgar, proprietor of *The Boston Store* in the town of Brockton, Massachusetts. In 1890, he dressed up as Santa Claus to amuse his customers during the pre-Christmas shopping season. This Santa Claus impersonator became the ancestor of a long line of department-store Santas. Today, they can still be found holding excited children on their knees and listening to the children's wish lists of Christmas presents in the days preceding Christmas.

In the early part of the 20th century, there were few high-quality Santa costumes available to those who wanted to follow James Edgar's example. Cheap

THE FEEL-GOOD FACTOR

Sundblom's Coca-Cola Santa was certainly eye-catching, but he also served another, less obvious purpose. He made his first appearance at a time when the United States was in the grip of the Great Depression, suffering poverty and unemployment on a massive scale. On city streets, stores still filled their windows with seasonal gifts and decorations, but there were also long lines of hungry people whose only meal of the day came from public soup kitchens. Street corners were still occupied by Santa Clauses ringing their bells for coins, but many of these charity collectors were ragged and needy-looking under their false beards and ill-fitting costumes.

The Coca-Cola company's symbolic Santa worked against these gloomy social realities by associating their product with happiness and good times. Sundblom delivered a fat, sleek, twinkling figure who radiated prosperity and a sense of well-being.

papier-mâché or waxed-cloth masks, imported from Germany, projected the face of a Santa who was more frightening than he was jovial, with huge, staring eyeholes and lurid, red-stained lips. These masks, mainly purchased for use at

Two Florida toddlers, dressed in red and white to echo the modern Santa's own costume, show little Christmas spirit when forced to pose for a holiday portrait.

FESTIVALS

family festivities, were combined with skimpy cloaks or robes made from red felt or muslin, which were padded out with a pillow or cushion. Beards were constructed from fluffy blobs of cotton, but it was also possible to buy a simple Santa hat with white whiskers already attached.

Such flimsy finery might have been good enough for domestic entertainments, but the department stores aspired to higher standards. To meet their exacting requirements, Santa Claus schools sprang up in New York and elsewhere, teaching the tricks of the trade, with special emphasis on dressing in the correct costume.

No Santa worth his reindeer was allowed to operate without a display of flowing white beard, mustache, and bushy eyebrows to match. Everything had to be either real—putting a premium on those men able to grow luxuriant facial hair in a properly snowy shade—or highly realistic. Naturally beardless Santas had to resort to securely glued-on sets of stage whiskers (the Santa school recommended those made of yak hair as the best for the job). Another requirement was a fine, fat, round belly. Those not favored by nature with enough flesh in the right places were advised to use a foam-rubber version. It was more realistic than a hidden cushion and less likely to collapse under the pressure of an endless stream of bouncing youngsters.

As the century progressed, Santa Claus' appearance became so firmly fixed in the collective imagination that it seemed acceptable to take some liberties. A 1951 edition of *Life* magazine showed him in Western guise, with a Stetson hat and high-heeled cowboy boots. And by the 1990s, the image of Santa reflected the diversity of the American population, with reported sightings of female Santas, African-American and Latino Santas, and Santas delivering their holiday greetings in sign language.

Other nations have made their own adaptations. During a recent Christmas season in Australia, a water-skiing Santa Claus skimmed down a river wearing red trunks and a white beard. In Japan, a Santa Claus dressed as Colonel Sanders was

SANTA CLAUS

At a Colorado aquarium, a helmeted and goggled Santa wears a completely waterproof version of the classic fur-trimmed suit. He holds out a card with a Christmas message on behalf of his fish companions.

seen selling fast food in a local outlet of Kentucky Fried Chicken, and a female Santa, in an adaptation of the classic red-and-white costume, has appeared on a railway poster announcing certain service changes during the Christmas season. The old, bearded wintertime visitor may have undergone countless transformations, but all over the world, no matter what costume he wears, Santa Claus still carries his gifts and delivers seasonal messages—with miraculous speed and efficiency.

CHAPTER 3

Halloween

Americans do not seem to be able to get enough of Halloween. It is estimated that U.S. households spend around $6.9 billion every year on costumes, cards, candies, pumpkins, party goods, and suitably spooky decorations for their houses.

While surfing the Internet for the perfect witch's hat or hanging plastic skeletons on their front porches, people may not realize that Halloween has its origins in religious rites and tribal customs practiced 2,000 years ago by the Celtic peoples of northwestern Europe.

This fall holiday is the descendant of the ancient Celtic fire festival called Samhain. According to the Celtic calendar, the night of October 31 and the first day of November marked the turning of the year. In the windswept islands and rocky peninsulas of Scotland, Ireland, Wales,

A white-robed Druid (left), reviving ritual practices believed to go back to the pre-Christian Celts, worships the sun at an ancient stone circle. The Halloween custom of bobbing for apples (right) is also thought to have Celtic roots.

and Brittany, this was the season after the last of the harvest was gathered, when the days grew shorter and the winter chill began to bite. To mark this transition, communities built huge ceremonial bonfires. Druid priests performed sacrificial rites to gain divine protection during the harsh months to come. It was the point in the annual cycle when supernatural forces were at their strongest. People sensed the presence of ghosts and spirits—those of their departed loved ones, as well as the unseen forms of unearthly entities.

Individuals gifted with prophetic powers regarded Samhain as the perfect moment to peer into the future. And anyone wishing to stay on the good side of fairies, elves, and other inhabitants of the invisible world made sure to leave offerings of food on their doorsteps. This was considered a prudent practice at any time of year, but at a time when the air was thick with spirits, householders would do anything to keep them happy—and keep them out.

ROMAN ROOTS

During the first century A.D, the Celtic world came under the influence of the Roman Empire. As Roman soldiers spread through France, colonized England, and struggled to extend their dominion into the Scottish moorlands and mountains farther north, they brought not only roads and the Latin language, but also their seasonal feasts and holy days. Two of these gradually merged with the old Samhain rites. Like the Celts, Romans honored the spirits of their dead with a holiday in late October. Another day in the same season was dedicated to Pomona, a goddess associated with trees and fruits, especially the apples of the fall. The modern custom of bobbing for apples at Halloween parties may be a remnant of old ritual tributes to Pomona.

CHRISTIAN RITES

Christianity, born in the era when the Roman Empire reached its height, took several hundred years to establish itself throughout Western Europe. Sacred

HALLOWEEN

bonfires gave way to chapels; Druids vanished and were replaced by priests of a different faith. To win the hearts and minds of Celtic and Roman believers, the Christian church adapted many of their old rites and sacred traditions.

By the beginning of the 11th century, a series of **papal decrees** had transformed and extended the old Celtic New Year celebrations. Instead of the wandering inhabitants of the spirit world, Christian martyrs and miracle workers became the objects of attention for the fall feast. It was no coincidence that many of their characteristics and special powers echoed those of the Celtic and Roman deities they replaced. In their honor, November 1 was designated "All Saints' Day"—or All-Hallowmas. The preceding night, October 31, was converted from the old fire festival of Samhain into the vigil known as All

While most Halloween imagery depicts witches dressed entirely in black, the cheerful crone on this early 20th-century postcard sports a red dress and ribbons on her pointed hat.

FESTIVALS

Hallows' Eve, or Halloween. Finally, the day following the Feast of All Saints, November 2, became All Souls' Day, dedicated to the known and unknown dead. In parts of the British Isles, this festival was marked by processions moving from house to house, offering to pray for the souls of any deceased family members, and receiving specially baked "soul cakes" as a token of appreciation for this service.

As these pagan and Christian practices merged and mutated, they gave birth to the modern, secular Halloween. Beliefs may have changed, and the names of the old gods are all but forgotten, but underneath the glossy, contemporary trappings, the customs and spirit of the old Samhain and All Hallows' Eve still survive.

DRESSING UP

Certain traditions are reflected between these old fall festivals and the present day. Bowls of food put out for Celtic fairies and soul cakes traded for a neighbor's prayers are mirrored in the candy bars handed out to trick-or-

Giant jack o'lanterns carved from pumpkins are a favorite Halloween house decoration. Smaller plastic ones make classic accessories for costumed trick-or-treaters, supplied with handles to carry candy or equipped with small battery-powered lights.

treaters. Images of witches, broomsticks, black cats, ghosts, and cobwebs imprinted on shopping bags and plastered across windows reflect dark northern nights when everyone knew that the spirits walked. Candles gleaming inside a jack-o'-lantern recall, however faintly, the blaze of a giant bonfire on a Scottish hill. But of all the time-honored customs still practiced on this night, nothing symbolizes Halloween so strongly as the wearing of masks and costumes.

It is impossible to put a date on such an old tradition. Some writers suggest that the practice can be traced back to the wearing of animal skins and masks during Druidical rites, or to an old folk belief that ashes from the Samhain bonfire, smeared on the face, would make the wearer invisible to unfriendly spirits. It is a matter of record that costumed revelers—known as "guisers"—took part in the Halloween celebrations at Scotland's royal palace of Holyrood in 1585. The report of these festivities gives no indication that there was anything particularly new or surprising about people turning up in costumes on this particular night of the year.

The costumes donned for a royal Halloween party were doubtless far more elaborate than those worn by the youths who cavorted across the Scottish and Irish countryside during the next 300 years' worth of Halloweens. A few daubs of ash from the fire, an old torn sheet, and a rough attempt at a homemade mask (known in Scots as a "fausse face") sufficed to turn village guisers into ghouls and ghosts, to amuse—or terrify—their neighbors.

OLD TRADITIONS IN A NEW WORLD

In the mid-19th century, when poverty and famine drove thousands of Irish peasants and Scottish laborers across the Atlantic to seek their fortunes in America, they brought their love of Halloween with them. Just as in the old country, playing pranks on neighbors was part of the fun. More than one hapless family woke up on the morning of November 1 to find that unseen tricksters had knocked over their wooden outhouse during the night.

FESTIVALS

> ### JACK-O'-LANTERN
> In Scotland and Ireland, Halloween revelers had traditionally illuminated their midnight wanderings by carving giant turnips, known as neeps, into candleholders. The New World provided a bigger and better fruit alternative, in the form of its orange pumpkins. As American popular culture has spread across the world, U.S. Halloween traditions are rapidly displacing local customs, even in those Celtic lands where the ancient festival was born. Slowly but surely, the grinning jack-o'-lantern is taking over from the neep.

The ways in which Americans mark the occasion have also changed dramatically. In the early 1900s, the most common form of Halloween celebration was a party. Most of these were informal get-togethers. Friends and family members made homemade costumes, ducked for apples, told ghost stories, and played fortune-telling games. Techniques for predicting the names, or at least the initials, of future marriage partners were particularly popular among young girls.

1920s AND 1930s

During the 1920s and 1930s, Halloween was regarded as an event for grown-ups. Rich city dwellers and their suburban counterparts held elaborate costume parties in hotels and country clubs. Often, these were organized around a specific theme, and participants rented costumes, or had them specially made, in keeping with the chosen subject for the night. The most popular themes were those that lent themselves to imaginative or extravagant dressing up, such as "The Last Days of the Roman Empire," with **togas** and garlands of laurel leaves, or "The Animal Kingdom," in all its feathered, furred, and scaly glory.

HALLOWEEN

Most Americans had neither the money nor the social contacts to buy their way into these glittering events, especially after the 1929 stock market crash and the Depression that followed. Instead, they took part in public celebrations—parades, costume contests, and other festivities—which were sponsored by towns or community groups.

1940s

In the 1940s, these communal events faded away, and Halloween became almost exclusively a children's activity. From 1941 through 1945, the United States was engaged in World War II. Its adult citizens had more frightening things to think about than witches and ghosts. When peace returned, family became a top priority: reunited sweethearts married, and long-postponed plans for having children were put into action. The result was a social phenomenon that began in the late 1940s and lasted until the beginning of the 1960s: the baby boom. As the numbers of children expanded, Halloween soon became equated almost entirely with the young.

Fancy-dress balls, or costume parties, were popular adult entertainment during the Roaring Twenties. This trio's headgear ranges from the comically spooky witch's hat to a sinister copy of the hoods worn by the racist vigilantes of the Ku Klux Klan.

At this point, Halloween centered on the practice of trick-or-treating, with neighborhood children going from door to door demanding candy. Essentially, the ritual was a form of friendly blackmail: the "treats" provided immunity against such "tricks" as a front lawn festooned with yards of toilet paper.

Over the next few decades, the custom itself would change in ways that reflected certain changes in society at large. In many parts of the country, parents became worried about their children's safety on Halloween night. There were many more cars on the road, and frightening reports of increased crime. So instead of allowing children out on their own or with small groups of friends their own age, many adults now escorted them from door to door, or limited trick-or-treating strictly to the houses of relatives and friends. Private Halloween parties, at home or school, became more popular than ever.

HOMEMADE COSTUMES

One thing did not change. The costumes worn for Halloween have remained just as important and exciting as the collection of chocolate bars, lollipops, candy corn, and other sugary treats.

Some families followed the old tradition of making costumes at home, using their ingenuity and whatever scrap materials were on hand. Supernatural themes were popular, as well as easy to make. A bed sheet, with appropriately positioned eyeholes, made a perfect ghost. It was

The costumes worn by this band of neighborhood trick-or-treaters run the gamut from cleverly improvised homemade outfits to store-bought creations on themes that range from circus clowns to classic witches.

HALLOWEEN

This advertisement for Woolworth's offers Halloween disguises inspired by such cartoon celebrities as Donald Duck and Bugs Bunny, as well as Howdy Doody, the puppet-presenter of a popular TV show.

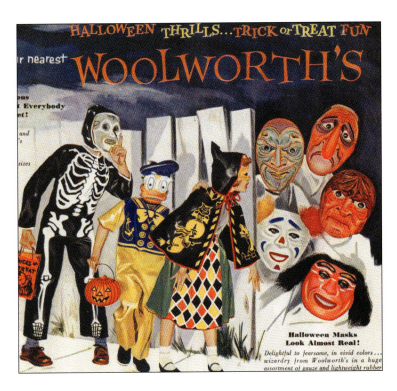

also roomy enough to conceal sweaters, scarves, and a jacket, thus solving the problem of keeping a trick-or-treater warm on a cold night without spoiling the effect of the costume. Households lucky enough to possess a dressing-up box full of old clothing, plus a parent who knew how to use a sewing machine, could fulfill any number of youthful fantasies, from a princess to a pirate.

COMMERCIAL COSTUMES

Meanwhile, the toy industry realized that there were vast profits to be made from the sale of colorful Halloween disguises. A handful of specialized costume manufacturers came to dominate the market, defining the styles seen on Halloween doorsteps for the rest of the century. Some of their products reflected familiar Halloween traditions—kits containing all the necessary garments, masks, and accessories for the well-dressed witch, ghoul, or goblin. Others were the classic outfits worn for costume parties or school plays all year-round: animal outfits, old-fashioned military uniforms, fur-trimmed royal robes and crowns, or apparel associated with well-known storybook characters, such as Little Red Riding Hood.

FESTIVALS

REFLECTIONS OF POPULAR CULTURE: RADIO AND TV

Almost as soon as they appeared in the stores, commercial costumes became reflections of the ever-shifting fads and fashions of American popular culture. In the late 1930s and 1940s, Halloween masqueraders dressed up as characters from their favorite radio programs and newspaper comic strips, such as Little Orphan Annie, Barney Google, or the hillbilly sweethearts from Dogpatch, L'il Abner and Daisy Mae. By the late 1950s, virtually every house had a television set. New costume ideas came pouring out of the little glass screen in the corner of the living room, honoring cartoon figures from children's daytime programs: Tom and Jerry, Winky-Dink, Huckleberry Hound, the Lone Ranger, and many more, as well as replicas of such flesh-and-blood stars as the red-headed comedienne Lucille Ball, star of the ever-popular *I Love Lucy* show, and television presenter Captain Kangaroo.

A larger-than-life Uncle Sam, with the Stars and Stripes emblazoned on his massive hat, greets his fellow citizens during the annual Halloween Parade in New York City's Greenwich Village.

POLITICS

The political traumas and great social and cultural changes of the 1960s were duly represented in the costumes of that decade's Halloweens. A politically aware trick-or-treater could dress up as President John F. Kennedy or his elegant First Lady, with carefully molded rubber masks to complete the effect. Kennedy's assassination in November 1963 put an end to that particular product's popularity, but outfits and masks representing famous political figures became part of the costume makers' inventory.

When the Vietnam War broke out, even trick-or-treaters took sides. Available costumes included Green Beret uniforms and rainbow-colored hippie **caftans**, complete with beads and dangling peace-symbol medallions. Although young children may not have had any opinions about the war, their teenage brothers and sisters, and their parents, certainly did. Some families bought these costumes simply because they liked the color or the design, but others saw them as a way to make a political statement.

ROCK 'N' ROLL ICONS AND MOVIE STARS

Music-loving teens could transform themselves into rock 'n' roll superstars, such as the Beatles—first with collarless suits and mop-top wigs, and later with the eccentric gold-braided uniforms from "Sergeant Pepper's Lonely Hearts Club Band." Meanwhile, their younger siblings dressed up as favorite toys: GI Joe, Action Man, or Barbie.

By the 1970s, the giant entertainment companies—creators of the nation's favorite television cartoons, Hollywood movies, and rock bands—realized that costumes were an excellent way to promote their products. Because of copyright laws, costume manufacturers needed permission to reproduce those images and had to pay the original creators. This arrangement suited both sides. The entertainment industry earned extra profits from selling the rights, and the costume makers had a guaranteed market for their goods—the hundreds of

> **RISING FROM THE ASHES**
>
> In the fall of 2001, shortly after the terrorist attack that destroyed the World Trade Center, people wondered if anyone could face the thought of a Halloween celebration in a traumatized city, just a short distance away from the scene of devastation. But the organizers, and the people of Greenwich Village, recalled the mythological bird called the phoenix. According to the ancient Greeks, this magical creature—even when destroyed in a fire—had the power to reappear, reborn and perfectly unscathed, from the ashes. So the Halloween parade went ahead, under the slogan "The Phoenix Has Risen."
>
> In a way, the wheel had turned full circle. Just as the ancient Samhain bonfires promised light in the winter darkness, and the medieval All Saints' and All Souls' Days remembered and honored the dead, so this newest Halloween custom gave people, even in a dark time, cause for hope and reason for celebration.

thousands of fans who wanted to spend Halloween night as a Bionic Woman, a Jedi warrior, a rock star, or the giant shark from the movie *Jaws*.

Throughout the rest of the century and beyond, this relationship between Halloween and popular culture would grow ever stronger. Although many creative individuals still preferred to turn old party dresses into silk and velvet vampire capes or construct one-of-a-kind outfits from recycled plastic and paper, they were likely to be outnumbered at many Halloween celebrations by replicas of that year's top singers and action-movie heroes.

HALLOWEEN PARADES

Meanwhile, other social changes were taking place. Even if Halloween no longer saw hordes of tiny costumed trick-or-treaters wandering unchaperoned through the streets, people still wanted to make the occasion special. Once again, public Halloween festivities became popular, especially in large cities. These events were not just for children, but included participants of all ages.

One of the most successful of these events is the Halloween parade held in New York City's Greenwich Village. Traditionally, this neighborhood has been a gathering place for artists, writers, theater people, and nonconformists of all kinds. In 1974, a local theater director and mask maker named Ralph Lee assembled a group of like-minded friends, who decided to create a unique celebration for this unique community.

The parade began as a street party and procession involving a handful of creative locals sporting weird and wonderful costumes, but it has expanded beyond all recognition. By the 1990s, television crews and film units from all over the world were descending on the Village to film tens of thousands of paraders, watched by over a million spectators. Even if they are not in the parades themselves, people get into the spirit of the day, wearing fancy costumes and face masks to compare with those in the passing parade. The cast of characters is almost endless, and the display of ingenuity unforgettable: the crew of the Starship Enterprise; the Easter Bunny; Dorothy, Toto, and her friends from *The Wizard of Oz*; a little troop of larger-than-life lipsticks, with tall, scarlet headpieces and silver-tube costumes; a walking clothesline; a 6-foot (183-cm) clove of garlic; and a gigantic slice of pizza, complete with extra anchovies and cheese.

This new tradition is intended to celebrate the rich diversity of Greenwich Village and the people of New York City as a whole, whatever their age group, ethnic background, sexual orientation, or physical abilities. Musicians of all kinds—from Jamaican reggae artists to Jewish **klezmer** bands to Scottish bagpipers—provide a background for this public event, which is not only an update of the community parties and parades of the early 1900s, but a vibrant expression of the spirit of New York.

CHAPTER 4

Festivals Around the World

All across the world, people enjoy the chance to change their appearance and become someone—or something—completely different, even if only for an hour or a day.

In virtually any continent, at any season of the year, someone somewhere is putting on a colorful disguise, donning a mask, or adorning face and body with symbolic markings and traditional decorations. The global calendar is full of

A Bulgarian man (left) wears a shaggy sheepskin suit as part of the festival of Kukeri. A Eastern European woman (right) wears traditional folk costume to celebrate a national holiday.

FESTIVALS

special days when dressing up is allowed, encouraged, or sometimes even required. The reason for the event may be a national or local holiday, a **rite of passage**, a religious festival, the commemoration of a historical event, a cultural celebration, or simply a good excuse to have fun.

CHANGING SEASONS

Rituals to mark the changing seasons of the year take place in many agricultural societies. Some go back thousands of years, to an age when the earliest farmers first learned the secrets of raising crops. They knew their survival depended on many things beyond their control, such as the weather, the health of their animals and plants, and the fertility of the soil. In hopes of pleasing the gods of nature, they performed ceremonies, made offerings of food, sacrificed livestock—or, in some cases, human beings—and dressed themselves in special masks or garments to imitate or impress the unseen powers.

THE KUKERI

In an age of advanced technology, city dwellers have long forgotten this sense of vulnerability and the rituals that their ancestors used against it. But in some rural areas, remnants of these practices are still alive, even if their origins are uncertain. One of the most dramatic of these seasonal rituals takes place in the Balkan mountains of southeastern Europe, in the remote

FESTIVALS AROUND THE WORLD

rural villages of Bulgaria. The festival of Kukeri is believed to combine early Christian beliefs with pagan traditions of the ancient Greeks.

At the end of the winter—just before the beginning of Lent in the Christian calendar—the ritual **mummers** called Kukeri make their appearance in the remotest settlements. These all-male groups wear shaggy sheepskin suits, belts adorned with copper bells, and frightful masks covered with elaborate beadwork, tassels, multicolored ribbons, and tufts of fur. Their leaders dance with strange swaying, lumbering steps, believed to imitate the nodding movement of wheat bearing plenty of grain. The clangor of the bells on their belts is thought to chase away the ghosts and evil spirits that cause famine and disease.

GEEREWOLDE

In addition to marking crucial turning points in the agricultural year, costumes play an important part in rituals marking important stages in the lives of human beings. One of the most visually exciting and dramatic festivals of this kind takes place in West Africa, among the Wodaabe people, a nomadic tribe that travels with its herds of cattle through Niger and neighboring regions. During the rainy season, when there is plenty of lush grass to feed everybody's animals, the whole scattered community comes together for the weeklong festival of Geerewolde. This social event is eagerly anticipated, as it gives people who spend most of the year in isolated family groups a chance to catch up with friends and relatives. But its most important purpose is as a ritual

The tall, tapered hoods worn by members of a Catholic brotherhood of penitents make an eerie spectacle against the sky in the Spanish city of Seville. The group is taking part in a solemn procession during Holy Week.

enabling the young men and women of the tribe to meet and choose their future marriage partners.

The Wodaabe place a high value on physical beauty, and have definite ideas about the features that make people attractive to the opposite sex. During the rest of the year, everyone dresses simply, in plain cotton garments without many ornaments. But when they come to the Geerewolde, the young men of the community spend hours each day transforming and adorning themselves from top to toe—hoping to catch the eye, and meet the exacting standards, of prospective brides. Every day throughout the festival, they dance before the young women, and each of these performances requires a different costume.

The preparations are just as dramatic as the dances themselves. To emphasize the length and elegance of their foreheads, the young men shave inches off their hairlines and braid the long hair that remains into elaborate **coiffures**. They use cosmetics with the care and skill of a Hollywood makeup artist. Black lines of kohl surround their eyes; rich color highlights their lips; a bright yellow paste serves as a background for patterned dots and circles in red and white; and white vertical lines painted down the nose emphasize its elegant slenderness and length.

The basic elements for each dance costume are richly varied, but include kilts of lustrous tanned leather over finely embroidered silken **tunics**. Headgear varies, from conical, lampshade-like hats to imposing white turbans topped with black ostrich feathers and adorned with dangling metalwork, beaded straps, and colorful plastic trinkets, such as key chains purchased in village markets.

Once these decorations are in place, the young men dance, using exaggerated eye movements and witty facial expressions to delight and fascinate the crowds of female onlookers. The young women in the audience have also taken pains to look their best. Embroidered skirts flash fragments of mirror glass; thick, brass leg bracelets rise from ankle to knee; ears display rows of brass earrings; large, ornately carved metal hairpins top complicated hairdos; and brightly striped headcloths are festooned with glittering decorations. And at

FESTIVALS AROUND THE WORLD

some point in the festivities, in between readjusting their hairdos and rearranging their jewelry, both sides will find time to make the right connections and fall in love.

SEMANA SANTA

Not all costume rituals involve such an explosion of ornament and color. Some derive their visual drama from dress that is stark, simple, and severe. Among the most memorable events in the Roman Catholic calendar, for instance, are the processions held in Seville and other cities of southern Spain during the "Semana Santa," or Holy Week, preceding Easter.

To celebrate the holiday Purim, commemorating the heroism of an ancient Jewish queen, young residents of Jerusalem parade in costume. The girl in red follows an old tradition by dressing as the queen from the story.

During these parades, floats holding ornate religious images are carried through the streets on the shoulders of sweating men, escorted by fraternities of black-robed male worshippers who veil their faces with thick masks pierced only by eyeholes and topped with tall, conical hoods.

These garments have remained unchanged for centuries, since the days when the religious officials of the Spanish Inquisition ruled with a heavy hand. To Americans aware of the grimmer aspects of their own country's history, these vestments may look strangely familiar. Because they concealed their wearers' appearances so effectively, members of the Ku Klux Klan wore versions of these garments for racist attacks and secret ceremonies. But such a connection is unknown to the members of these Spanish religious fraternities, who wear their Semana Santa robes and face coverings as a mark of spiritual devotion.

CORPUS CHRISTI

Religiously inspired festival costumes are not always quite so somber. In contrast to the timeless image of cowled and hooded figures bearing enthroned statues through the Spanish streets, the Corpus Christi ceremonies in Mexico City have become an upbeat, Hispanic Christian counterpart of Halloween. Children attending Mass on this important Christian feast day are encouraged to come to the service in colorful costumes. The cathedral is filled with rows of pint-size space travelers, kindergarten cowboys, and little girls in miniature versions of authentic regional dress.

PURIM

The Jewish calendar also includes a holiday when children's costumes are an integral part of the festivities. The spring festival of Purim commemorates a narrative harking back to Biblical times, concerning the King of Persia's Jewish consort, Queen Esther. She discovered that a hostile court official was plotting to exterminate all the Jews in the realm, and managed to persuade her royal spouse

FESTIVALS AROUND THE WORLD

to prevent the slaughter and hang the would-be murderer instead. Celebrations traditionally include high-spirited costume parties where children dress up as the main characters in the story—as Esther herself, her pious cousin Mordecai, or Ahasuerus, the Persian king. Costumes are often improvised for the occasion, relying on spare tablecloths, faded bath towels, old curtains, and foil crowns.

THE KYOTO FESTIVAL

Costume rituals are also used to celebrate the history and culture of entire nations or individual communities. In Kyoto, Japan, a spectacular festival is held every October to commemorate the era when this ancient city was Japan's imperial capital. The event has been a high point in the national calendar since 1895, and it features a parade with costumes representing different historical periods. As the procession wends its way from an old city gate to the tombs of the emperors of the medieval Heian Period, participants—on foot and on horseback—display the 12-layered, multicolored silk robes of 10th-century court ladies, the armored suits of samurai warriors from the 1500s, or the brilliantly patterned kimono and broad, embroidered sashes typical of the Edo Period, which lasted from the 17th to the 19th centuries.

THE ENGLISH PEARLIES

The enthusiasm for reviving costumes of bygone days is also popular in England. One group of proud Londoners, for example, turns out on such special

The peaked cap, vest, and neckerchief of this "Pearly King" were typical of English workingmen in the early 1900s.

57

occasions as the festive Derby Day at Epsom Races wearing costumes completely encrusted with tiny pearl buttons. Known as the Pearlies, or the Pearly Kings and Queens, they are the descendants of the cockney apple vendors, or costermongers, who sold their wares for centuries in the city's streets and markets.

There are different Pearlie tribes and families, each with its own lovingly preserved set of costumes. Members of these groups are protective of the right to wear these suits. They generally consist of black trousers and jackets for the men, and skirts and long, wide-lapeled jackets for the women. Clothes for both sexes are cut according to the early 20th-century tailoring fashions popular until the end of the 1930s. Seams, cuffs, and surfaces are entirely covered with swirling rings and rows of identical pearl buttons. The female Pearlies crown their costumes with a hat topped by plumes of multicolored ostrich feathers, which was regulation headgear for ladies attending the royal court from Queen Victoria's reign until the outbreak of World War II.

UP-HELLY-AA

Another, very different historical costume tradition flourishes at the opposite end of the British Isles, in Shetland, that group of North Sea islands located between Scotland and Norway. In some ways, culturally as well as geographically, Shetlanders feel closer to the Norwegians than they do to their fellow Scots. Ownership of the isles passed from the Norse kings to Scotland's sovereigns sometime in the late 1400s—a short time span for a place where settlements can be traced back to at least the second millennium B.C.

To celebrate this heritage and cheer themselves up during the almost-continuous darkness of the winter months, Shetlanders hold a modern equivalent of the ancient Yule fire festivals every January, known by the dialect name of Up-Helly-Aa. Preparations for the festivities can take months—including the time it takes for people to grow their beards and hair long enough to pass for suitably whiskery figures from the darkest medieval days. The event features a huge ceremonial procession, with a replica of a Viking longship dragged through the streets to the harbor. Pulling the longship are squads of brawny, bearded men in highly stylized Viking costume, complete with shaggy woolen cloaks, horned or winged helmets, battle axes, and circular shields. Hundreds of marchers, also in costume and carrying blazing torches, accompany the vessel on its journey. The climax of the parade comes when the longship is launched and the "Vikings" toss their hundreds of burning brands onto its decks, setting the craft on fire. Flames light up the night until the boat is nothing more than a charred hulk floating on the oil-black waters.

Men from the Shetland Isles, north of Scotland, spend months cultivating suitably Viking-style beards to complete their costume for the winter fire-festival, Up-Helly-Aa.

GLOSSARY

Abstinence the voluntary giving up of certain foods, drinks, or other pleasures

Breeches short pants covering the hips and thighs and fitting snugly at the lower edges at or just below the knee

Caftan a long, flowing garment, often with a belt, used by men and some women in Middle Eastern and other cultures, which was adapted in the West in the 1960s and 1970s as an item of hippie costume

Caricature exaggeration by means of often ludicrous distortion of parts or characteristics

Coiffure a style of arranging the hair

Courtier one in attendance at a royal court

Crinoline a full, stiff underskirt

Gargoyles grotesque carved-stone figures mixing human and animal traits, serving as rainwater spouts on the roofs of medieval churches

Klezmer a form of traditional popular music used for weddings and other celebrations by Jews of Eastern European origin

Krewes members-only social clubs that march together in costume at the New Orleans Mardi Gras

Latrine a receptacle for use as a toilet

Mummers costumed actors in folk plays or other traditional local rituals, often using masks and mime

Papal decree an official ruling made by the Pope as head of the Roman Catholic Church

Pious showing reverence for deity and devotion to divine worship

Raiment clothing

Regalia symbolic objects representing royal or other forms of official power

Rite of passage a ritual or ceremony used by members of a particular culture to mark important stages in human life, such as coming-of-age or a religious confirmation

Satire a piece of writing or other form of art using humor to mock and criticize the behavior of individuals, groups, or society as a whole

Saturnalia ancient Roman festival honoring the god Saturn, featuring wild merrymaking and misbehavior

Satyrs imaginary forest creatures in Greek and Roman mythology, half-human and half-goat, with shaggy hindquarters and hooves

Segregation the separation of a race, class, or ethnic group from others by discriminatory means

Toga loose, flowing garment consisting of

GLOSSARY/TIMELINE

a single piece of cloth, worn wrapped around the body

Tunic one-piece garment, sometimes loose and sleeveless

Venerable distinguished; deserving of honor and respect through age or achievements

TIMELINE

The Life and Times of Santa Claus

4th century A.D. The future Saint Nicholas is born in Lycia, Asia Minor (present-day Turkey), enters the Church, and eventually becomes Bishop of Myra.

9th century Methodius, Patriarch of Constantinople, writes *The Life of Saint Nicholas*, recounting his many miracles and acts of kindness.

1622 The establishment of the Dutch colony of New Amsterdam, later to become an English colony and renamed New York; settlers from the Netherlands bring their Christmas customs, including the tradition that Saint Nicholas, known as Sinterklaas, is the deliverer of seasonal gifts to deserving children.

1809 The American writer Washington Irving, author of *Rip Van Winkle,* begins publishing nostalgic tales based on the old Dutch colony, triggering a revival of interest in New Amsterdam life and folk traditions.

1823 Publication of the poem *The Night Before Christmas* by Clement Clark Moore.

1866 Cartoonist Thomas Nast draws the image that becomes the prototype for the modern face of Santa Claus.

1890 James Edgar, owner of The Boston Store in Brockton, Massachusetts, dresses up in a Santa costume to entertain his customers during the Christmas shopping season, pioneering the concept of the department-store Santa Claus.

1897 The image of Santa is used in an advertisement for Pears Soap.

1902 Santa Claus advertises Waterman Pens.

1912 The first Santa Claus cover, by J. C. Leyendecker, appears on a Christmas issue of the *Saturday Evening Post* magazine, depicting an extremely thin and hungry-looking street-corner charity collector swamped by an oversize Santa costume.

1918 *The Saturday Evening Post* Christmas cover puts Santa into the uniform of the U.S. Army, which was fighting overseas in World War I.

1931 Santa Claus begins his long-term career as the Christmas face of Coca-Cola in a series of advertisements by commercial artist Haddon Sundblom.

FURTHER INFORMATION

BOOKS

Fisher, Angela. *Africa Adorned.* London: Collins, 1984.

Galembo, Phyllis et al. *Dressed for Thrills: 100 Years of Halloween Costumes and Masquerade.* New York: Harry N. Abrams, 2002.

Harrison, Shirley. *Who Is Father Christmas?* Newton Abbot, England: David and Charles, 1981.

Itasaka, Gem. *Japan: An Illustrated Encyclopedia.* Tokyo: Kodansha, 1993.

Kennett, Frances and Caroline Macdonald-Haig. *World Dress.* London: Mitchell-Beasley, 1994.

Kinser, Samuel. *Carnival American Style.* Chicago: University of Chicago Press, 1990.

Kugelmass, Jack. *Masked Culture: The Greenwich Village Halloween Parade.* New York: Columbia University Press, 1994.

Landau, Elaine. *Mardi Gras—Parades, Costumes, and Parties.* Berkeley Heights, NJ: Enslow Publishers, 2002.

MacDermott, Mercia. *Bulgarian Folk Customs.* London: Jessica Kingsley, 1998.

Marling, Karal Ann. *Merry Christmas! Celebrating America's Greatest Holiday.* Cambridge, Mass.: Harvard University Press, 2000.

Mason, Peter. *Bacchanal! The Carnival Culture of Trinidad.* Philadelphia: Temple University Press, 1998.

Miller, D. *Unwrapping Christmas.* Oxford: Clarendon Press, 1993.

Waits, William B. *The Modern Christmas in America.* New York: New York University Press, 1993.

Wilcox, R. T. *Folk and Festival Costumes of the World.* London: Batsford, 1989.

FURTHER INFORMATION

ONLINE SOURCES

Society and Culture in Andalucia
www.andalucia.com/culture/home.html
Andalucia in Southern Spain has a rich cultural heritage, which places much importance on its fiestas. Clicking the Festivals tab will give an explanation of the main ones. The Bullfighting link is also of interest, and includes a section on matador dress.

Haunted Homepage: Pumkin Patch
http://hometown.aol.com/airzinnn/Pumpkin_Patch.htm
The story of the jack o' lantern and a brief discussion about the origins of Halloween.

Mardi Gras Indians: Tradition and History
www.mardigrasindians.com
An interesting account of the Mardi Gras Indians: how the tradition began, and how things have changed today. Includes stunning examples of Madi Gras Indian costumes.

Up-Helly-Aa
www.up-helly-aa.org.uk
A history of this British fire festival is given, along with lyrics to some of the traditional festival songs, articles about the event from *The Shetland Times*, and links to other Viking sites.

ABOUT THE AUTHOR

Ellen Galford has written books and articles on many different aspects of social history, archaeology, and popular culture—covering such areas as folklore and mythology, food and cookery, comparative religion, crime, genealogy, and sport for a number of different American and British publishers. She has also written four novels, as well as short fiction and non-fiction pieces for several literary anthologies, and has written features and reviews for a variety of publications.

Ellen has worked as an editor on children's fiction and adult information books, and is currently a part-time college lecturer and occasional contributor to arts and current affairs programs for BBC Radio.

FESTIVALS

INDEX

References in italics refer to illustrations

accessories *15*, 26, *40*, 41, 53, 58 see also jewelry
advertisements 22, 29, 31, *45*
African Americans 14–15, 16, 17–18
beads *8*, 10, 21
beards 58, 59
    Santa Claus *22*, 23, 25, 28–9, *30*, 31, 32, 34
Brazil 21
Bulgaria *50*, 52–3

carnivals 10, 12–13 see also Mardi Gras
    balls 12, 14
    Brazilian 21
    European *11*, 21
    societies 12, 14, 16, 17–18, 20
    Trinidadian 20
Catholics see Christians
Celts *36*, 37–8, 39, 42
Christians *52–3*, 55–6
    carnivals 10, 12
    Christmas 25–6
    rites 38–40
Christmas 24, 25, 27
    gifts 26, 29, *30*, 32, 35
Coca-Cola company *22*, 31, 32
colors 20, 25, 26, 27, 29, 30, 34, *55*
cosmetics 54
costumes see also accessories; disguises; footwear; headgear
    bishop's robes 26, 27, 29
    carnivals 11, 20, 21
    Druids *36*
    embroidered 17, 54
    folk *51*
    Halloween *39*, 41, 44–6, 47
    Japanese 57
    Kukeri *50*, 53
    Mardi Gras 16, 17
    Native American 17–18, 19
    Pearly King *57*, 58
    Santa Claus 26, *28*, 29, *30*, 31, 34–5
    Viking 59
    Wodaabe 54
culture
    balls *12*, 14, 42
    dancing 54
    popular 46, 47–8, 49
department stores 23, 26, 32, 34
disguises
    animals *12*, 13
    carnivals *12*, 14
    devils 20
    Halloween 45–8, 49
    Mardi Gras 9–10
    royalty 9, 13, 14, 15, 16
Druids *36*, 38, 39, 41
England 57–8
Europe *11*, 12–13, 21, 50, *51*, 52–3, 55–6 see also individual countries

fabrics
    cotton 54
    silk 54, 57
    velvet 30
face paints 21, 54
Father Christmas see Santa Claus
feathers 54, 58
festivals see also carnivals; Mardi Gras
    British 57–9
    European 50, *51*, 52–3, 55–6
    Japanese 57
    Jewish *55*, 56–7
    Mexican 56
    seasonal 24–5, 52–3, 58–9
    West African 53–5
floats 10, *15*
footwear *22*, 29, 30
France 13, 14
furs *15*, 28, 29, 30

Gay and Lesbian parade *18*
Germany 21
ghosts 13, 38, 41, 42, 44, 45, 53
hairstyles 21, 54, 58 see also beards
Halloween *37*, *39*, 40–4
    costumes 41, 44–6, 47
    decorations *40*, 41
    gifts 38, 40–1, 43–4, 45, 47
    parades 43, *46*, 48–9
headdresses
    crowns 13, *15*
    feathered 17, 18, 21
headgear
    caps 29, *57*
    hats 21, 34, 54, 58
    hoods *43*, *52–3*, 56
    miters 26, 27, 29
    witches *39*, *43*
horses 24, 26

Japan 57
jewelry *8*, 10, 54
Jews 55, 56–7

Ku Klux Klan *43*, 56

leather *22*, 29, 30, 54

Mardi Gras *8*, 9–10, 14–15, 16–19
masks 9, *11*, 53, 56
    carnivals *12*, 13
    gargoyle 20
    Halloween 41, 47, 49
    Santa Claus 33–4
masquerades see disguises
Mexico 56

Native Americans 17–18, 19
New Orleans *8*, 9–10, 14–15, 16–19
New York *46*, 48, 49

pagan rites 24–5, 53
    Druids *36*, 38, 41
    Halloween 37–8, 40
parades
    carnivals 10, 14, 15
    Halloween 43, *46*, 48–9
    Mardi Gras 9–10, 19
    Viking 59
processions, Christian *52–3*, 55–6 see also parades
pumpkins *40*, 41, 42

reindeer 24, 27
retail trade see department stores
Rome, ancient 10, 12, 38
royalty
    carnivals 9, 13, 14, 15, 16, 20
    festivals *55*, 56–7

Saint Nicholas *23*, 25–7, 29
Santa Claus *22*, 23–24, 25, 26, *33*
    department stores 32, 34
    gift bearers 24, 25, 26, 29, *30*
    images 28–31, 32, 34–5
Shetland Isles 58–9
sleighs 24, 27
Spain *52–3*, 55–6
spirits 38, 41, 53 see also ghosts
Swiss Guards 13

West Africa 53–5
witches *39*, *43*, 45